Away from Shore

Poems By

Mary McCormack Deka

Dedication

To my poetry teachers throughout the years: Kate Sullivan, Michael Madonick, Janice Harrington, and Brigit Kelly. I was so incredibly lucky to be in your classes.

Also to Grams, Kristen, Shikhank, Niketha, Kamilla, and Pickles. You have inspired and encouraged my poetry more than you might imagine.

To Grandma Emily. A poet herself.

To everyone who's ever read my work and given me feedback. Your interest and comments mean the world to me.

And to all of my family and friends. Your love is a blessing.

Contents

About the Author

Acknowledgments

The author thanks the editors of the journals and contests in which the following poems (some of which have been revised) have appeared or received recognition:

Bare Hands Poetry and Photography Postcard Competition 2013: "Folding, Unfolding";

Storm Cellar: "Feverish", "Here";

Desmond O'Grady Poetry Competition 2012 (Finalist): "Saved"

Preface

After I had my heart broken, I woke each morning with a headache, thinking, *What could I have done differently? Is there something I could have done? What could I have done differently?* Over and over again, the same thoughts, rephrased, getting me nowhere. But it's all I could think.

There was no way to escape heartbreak easily. It clutched onto me, and I had to fight to be myself again.

For any of you who've struggled, or are struggling, I hope these poems help you take heart. They share my story from the very beginning, when I was so much in love (simply holding hands a joy), to the end of the relationship, when I was distraught and confused and lost.

The first section is filled with poems of exuberance, curiosity, and love. In the second section, I grapple with a breakup. In the third section, I'm stuck between knowing things are over and wanting them to be as they were. In the fourth section, I begin to pull myself out of grief, come to terms with what I've lost, and seek out my dreams. The very last poems, in the fifth section, describe how I start to wake up to the world again, realizing how much it, and I, have to offer.

No one emotion can last forever. As endless as my despair seemed at one point, it too went away. There is always a reason to live, to survive the worst. Sometimes it just takes a single quiet moment—a moth lifting its wings in the grass—to remind us of that.

I

Flight

When he held my hand
for the first time
it was like I lifted
right off the ground—
the rest of the world so tiny
and insignificant.

A Wish

When it seemed
everyone else
had been kissed,
my lips only knew the touch
of water,
chaste,
pure.

It felt like winter,
my lips were so
parched, burning
to taste
that elixir,
love, the potion
whose one drop
is more powerful
than anything else
in the world.

I wished
to know love,
and got what I wished for,
learned how it takes
you over, how
it doesn't stop
at one kiss.

Sailing

Shooting stars—
hundreds and hundreds of them
like anchors being cast down
to keep the sky
from drifting away.
What ships go sailing
up there?

I wanted to explore this
with him. I wanted
to dodge across rooftops
with kites in our hands
so we could sail away ourselves
to join the universe.

We wove our lips together,
tucked shyness under the tongue.
His hand drew me closer.
My nose brushed his cheek.
Our eyes trembled shut.

And he and I floated
through the heavens. Purple
lilies on black sheets of sky.
Fish skipped past like stones on water.

We followed, tangled ourselves
to the stars, then fell, with them,
back into our bodies.

Mango

Sunset skin
lips lost in
starry strands
my tangled teeth
in his golden kiss
what a sweet
sweet lover
he was.

Of Silence, and Eyes

He said, *It looks like you have a jasmine
flower behind your ear.*

He said this although the jasmine flower
was really a piece of tissue paper
for soaking up wet earwax.

He brushed my cheeks with his finger,
kissed them. This when my cheeks were
red with a rash. He said, *Sit, I'll bring you
water. Rest.*

I was too sick to move, or speak,
but he understood. I smiled, though
my face was still.

I used that secret language of silence,
and eyes.

Together

Every morning I woke
dazzled. How the world
arched over us—
possibilities shimmering.
We were like two people emerging
from some dark tunnel
into a crystal cavern—
tentative, awed.

Fire

What was the red
of autumn leaves
next to the fire
of his gaze?

What was anything
compared to that?
He lit me up inside
with a kiss, held my heartstrings
in his fist.

To me, it was like the sun
rested in his eyes. I glowed
against his skin.

I took him with me,
like a lantern,
into the forest of my heart.
And I forgot
that he was made of fire,
that his touch
could make things burn.

II

Folding, Unfolding

He took his glasses off
at night,
folded them up,
placed them
on top of his textbooks.
He was gentle
with the frames,
each one a blade
of grass, a wing
slightly out of alignment.

He tried to be gentle
with me too,
folding and unfolding
his hands
as we sat together,
looking at me
in small glances.

I wanted to crumple
his words,
toss them away,
but he'd been so careful,
so precise
that they settled
in the creases of my palms
like origami cranes,
paper talons seeking
footholds.

Over

Things trotted along
until that day
when the hours and minutes
reared up around us
and his words—carefully
thought over—
struck me, flung me
from my senses,
dazed, wondering
what had happened,
if there was anything
I could have done.

Stone

He turned me
into a rabbit, a squirrel,
stock-still as he spoke,
each word another spell cast,
transforming my limbs,
numbing them
to stone.

And if he changed, too,
I was powerless to stop it,
watching from the ground
as he took off
with new swan's wings.
He looked beautiful
and distant. I tried calling him back,
but my mouth, too,
was numb.

I hoped
he would miss me
but knew he was gone,
different now, that he'd find another
creature of his own kind,
someone to fly with
through the cold
blue sky.

Quiet

My dreams
were like gardens
ransacked,
roses uprooted,
gone.
My mind
was like a city
pillaged,
bricks crumbled
into dust,
temples to him
abandoned.
But beneath
the rubble, I found
this little ditty,
a children's song
rising out of my chest.
If all the world
were apple pie...
It was a strange
comfort, like
the random
pattering
of a wood-
pecker's beak
when everything
else has gone
quiet.

Mirror

Into the mirror
I would escape, no need to explain
anything. I'd just vanish
into silver, the small suitcase of my past
gripped in my hand. I'd walk
right through
my own reflection.

He Said

He said listen, look at me, it'll be okay,
but there were secrets in my eyes so I
looked away.

He said hush, don't worry, you think too
much. I couldn't help it. I was hurting.
Thoughts come with touch.

He said if you need me, I'm still here
for you. But if there was another girl
with him, what would I do?

He said in a different life, in some other
age. My heart spun in circles, jumped out
of its cage. He said it would be easy

to be apart, it would be good to be free.
I loved him. I hated him. Couldn't he see
what he'd done to me?

He said he was all right; he'd hold up on
his own. I didn't say don't leave, I don't
want to be alone.

I said that's great. You're awesome.
You'll survive. I didn't say
I had a dragon curled up inside.

Midnight

Come midnight
I was deep in sleep,
lost in the realm
of shadow and wonder,
that strange carnival
where we try on
infinite masks,
journey to places
unknown, where we become
anything we dream.

It was hard to wake up.

How Remarkable It Is

How remarkable it is what we undergo

                  and how we are even
                      recognizable

           afterward
                  how we can
continue on   can live

as if we still feel

the flesh on our bones.

Alone

I wanted to be alone
with the wind,
just the wind.

Whittled Down

When you're whittled down
it's easier to snap,
it's easier to break
than to grow back
into who you were and are
and will be, always,
until you're gone.

When you're whittled down
you're sharper with your words
because it's a way to protect
what you have left,
and what you have left
is there behind your words:

the way you think,
the way you laugh,
the way you walk,
the things you can't say
because they're so much
a part of you
that how can you explain?

You can whittle down a person
to just about nothing,
but it doesn't change a thing,
really, about who
they are.

The Curse

You are so beautiful
eyes cling to you
like mussel shells
to rock.

Your smile is so sweet
it makes the fiercest man
nothing but a newborn
trembling lamb.

Your voice is so warm
it could tuck
children straight
into dreamy sleep.

Your eyes are two rivers
that offer peace
and mischief,
like brown trout, jumping.

You are wonderful, but
you don't see that. You just see
the face of the one
who left you.

The Edge of Night

When beyond the hills
the ocean was grey
and wild;
when the rivers
only dared whisper
and the sky was silent,
watchful;
when the moon
felt sorry enough
to light the way,
I had come to the edge
of sorrow, the edge
of night.

Step, I thought.
Let me step off this cliff, this despair,
fall and fall and fall
out of sorrow,
out of the world
if that's what it takes.

Fantasy

Sometimes, all I wanted to do
was step into a book and live
another person's life.

III

Feverish

The bone beneath my eye
was like a bowl.
And my eye the offering
inside.

Maybe the bone was a boat.
It bumped nose, found
no way out.

I swam dazed
alongside my eye bone.
My arms floundered
through water.
Thoughts scraped
my ribs.

I couldn't sleep.
My eyes jostled
in their sockets.
I sank into the pillow,
stared up.

From under my bed
came the knock of eyes
turned to marbles
that clattered
against each other
on the floorboards.

Saved

I was never baptized
unless in secret by a great aunt.
Strange, I dipped my fingers
in a glass of water, pressed them
to my forehead.
It glistened.

I touched my eye
through the eyelid.
The skin was soft
as an animal-skin sack
used to carry water.
I knew nothing
of carrying animal-skin sacks,
and thus, was fascinated.

What a haze I lived in.
But then the sky
was scraped clear of blue.
Everything was clear.
For example: stories
save people. I knew how
they pined away. Pine:
to be whittled down
to a stick of bone.

Some days
I had little desire
to clap, but then
I envisioned myself
onstage, everyone's eyes
taken up with me.
I swung in the curtains,
up and over the crowd
like a trapeze artist. I alighted
on a folding chair, balanced
like a flamingo.

Everyone else stood too,
on top of the chairs,
and we sang. Words winged up and up
so that to catch them you had to rise
and run about.

The Chance

It drove me
crazy,
kept me
from moving on,
the chance that maybe
you regretted
the breakup—
I knew, I knew
how unlikely that was,
but there was that tiniest of iotas
of chance
that you did,
and if I dropped by
you would say,
with an ache
in your voice,
*I was hoping
it was you.*
You would give me
a sunflower,
tell me
you loved me,
and…that's as far
as I imagined.

With You Again

My feet knew
where you lived,
so of course I went there,
couldn't help myself,
giddy to see you
after just a few weeks apart.

I knew it was over, we
were over, knew the worst
possible place to go
was into your arms, but oh,
my feet felt so light,
they carried me, they floated
like rose petals
in a fountain of water,
like the sun on the surface
of a wishing well.

They danced me
to your door, they made me
go there. Like red shoes in a fairy tale,
that won't stop waltzing,
my own feet would not stop.

They knew my wish,
and acted on it.
My feet took me to you,
and you held me. You held me.
And we kissed.

Bitter

Ever had a swig of milk,
gone sour? Or bitten into an apple,
soft? So different
from what you'd expected.
Startling. But I *knew*
it would be different,
so why was I surprised? How
could I have thought it would be
what it was before? I knew
our time had come and gone—
sour, soft.

I knew that each kiss, each caress
would be tainted, bitter
as an almond stuck in the throat.

The End

This can't go on
anymore, I said.
It's over,
it has to be over.
The words drifted
in the air
like ginkgo leaves,
the last remnants
of a time, dying,
our love floating to rest—
a blanket of gold
on the ground.

Love

Like an elephant
love is tender, lumbering.

Careful,
or it can knock you over.

IV

Under the Moon

Her hair turns silver;
she stands under the moon.
Each breath in leaves as a sigh,
under the moon.

What great mystery
in all that is quiet;
oh, to gaze at midnight sky
under the moon.

And love the greatest
mystery of them all.
She wants to ask questions, *why*,
under the moon.

Her thoughts are jumbled,
released after long days.
How easy it is to cry
under the moon.

Mary, lift each night
like elixir and tilt
into your throat its dark dye,
under the moon.

Moon

It doesn't matter
how much you scream
or weep, in the dark
the moon stays silent,
distant, bundled up
in a thick white blanket
that she wears
not for warmth
against the night sky,
but to muffle
the cries from earth.

Depression

Her stomach is taut, her breath trapped
in her lungs. She taps the beauty mark
on her wrist, but nothing happens.
Raindrops hang suspended
from the eaves.

The cobblestone street looks as usual—
full of puppeteers in their wacky
green caps, the one-eyed vendor
who sells hot chocolate with peppermint
or chilies,
the kids in bright swimsuits
headed to the seashore with shells
cupped in their palms like boats,
great wishes tucked inside.

The girl stares at them all and wonders
if they know. *But how could they?*
Pain laces through her, not dainty
like the frills on a fancy dress,
but sharp as the teeth of a saw,
ripping through trees.
Her head has oceans inside,
waiting to be cried.

How much longer can I go on?
A rabbit in a world of foxes.
A child lost in a happy crowd.
She stares a while longer, hoping

for someone to recognize her,
to smile, to invite her inside
for a family dinner around a hearth.
She'd be content with the sun
coming out.

When the sky stays grey, and the people
keep moving past,
she steps inside a small
antique store, is comforted
by the tinkling bell,
the shopkeeper's voice, and a strange red
and white rug in the center
of the floor, that to her eyes
looks like a herd of wild horses.

Phone Call, After the Breakup

Questions stampeded
through my body
even when it was clear
our conversation
was not one about truths
and feelings. It was the end
made more real, again,
by our clipped tones,
by the way his words fell heavy
into my consciousness
like stones into a well—
not all that significant,
but making ripples
nonetheless.

I held my tongue
to the roof of my mouth
like a barricade. My questions
turned, raced through my chest.
Then the talk ended
and everything was smooth again,
normal, but below the surface
lay cold rocks
that were not there before,
and were difficult
to dislodge.

Writing, After the Breakup

I left my thoughts
behind and watched
as one by one
sparrows lined up
on the telephone wire.
I wrote about *them*—
how still they are,
how slight their weight,
but how fast
their hearts must beat
in those tiny
feathered chests.

The White Peacock

A woman drove by
in a white car with a white peacock
in the passenger seat. She smoothed
her fingers over its feathers, gentle, as if
she were touching each of its eyes
to sleep.

Still

I picked up dried maple leaves,
watched clouds stretch across the sky.

I was still for minutes, hours,
alone with the grass, and the wind.

I wanted to be attuned
to those quiet things around us.

I, too, am quiet. I know how much it
means to find even just one listener.

Here

Ice broke into silk
and the sun spun
its strands, light-
handed as an old woman
at her loom. The sun
closed my eyes.

And without sight it was sound
that brought story. Sound
that pulled reeds up
through ripples, stretched arms out
until fingers touched sky, stars—*sitars,*
instruments whose strings
weave night
and day

together.

Pluck, and the moth-glow moon
hummed, hovered in air.

Pluck, and up leapt grasshoppers, up
leapt whistle from tongue.

Twigs bent. A blue jay's weight?
Calls resonated in the cold.

hee-u.

                              hee-u.
          akee aquí.
akee aquí.

In my eardrums:
hum whistle leap
crack split spool

In my mouth the words:
here. i'm here.

Choice

With his words of love
lifted like blinders
from the sides of my eyes,
there was choice again,
there were options
clear to me. The path was full
of everything I forgot to notice
when looking into his eyes.

Time

What had I been thinking?
All those days, all that time
I could have been
dancing! I could have been
traveling to Morocco
or Mongolia
or Brazil. I could've
gotten a job working with goats,
could've learned horseback riding.

Breakfast

Some people read tea leaves.
I read cereal flakes
stuck to the bottom of my bowl
after breakfast.
I read grapefruit pulp
beached on my plate
like pink birds.

You need to travel, I read,
more than anything.

Gallop

I woke in the morning,
and took a good look
at the ceiling—
a hardened field
covered with snow.
I heard hoof beats.
Those were my dreams,
galloping away.

I galloped after them.

V

Hitch-hiking

I had to get away, so I went
to Ireland.
I lived by a beach,
ran up and down hills
with two border collies,
tried a pint of hard cider,
and wrote letters to send back home.
I wore welly boots,
and hitched rides.
Sometimes the people who stopped
were women,
but mostly they were men.
One said the wellies I wore
were attractive; they showed
I'd be a hard-working wife.
He asked if I wanted to meet
for a drink that night. He wanted
to drop me off at my front door.
I told him the only way
to my house
was on foot. I had him stop
in front of green fields,
and then I got out,
slipped under a fence,
passed horses and farmhouses,
and left him to wonder
who the heck
was that beautiful,
fearless girl.

Free

Cast adrift,
without him
to anchor me,
I could have led
a wild life—
never in the same place
twice, a whirlwind girl,
ready to knock you
off your feet.

Hidden

When I got into town,
occasionally,
for an evening of live music,
or when I'd hitch rides
to the local tourist destinations,
people would be surprised
to learn I lived around there,
hidden among the flocks of sheep
and the mostly old,
bearded farmers.

Shy

My voice was a tightrope
made of a single spider's strand.

Delicate, stretched thin.

Sometimes, it just wanted to hide
in an aloe vera plant.

Lost Somewhere

I could have wandered
till sunrise, slept
on a cold rock, let my legs
go numb as my heart.
But instead I stood
at that door and I knocked;
I knocked; I knocked.
A seagull flapped from my throat,
then was lost somewhere
in the dark.

Fear quickened my breath
the way excitement does,
lungs tight in their box
of ribs.

The dark swallowed me whole,
like a Jonathan apple
gone into the mouth of a horse.
I waited there, inside the dark,
until someone opened
the door.

For the Horses

Every evening
I'd grab fistfuls of grass
for the horses.
They'd line up
by the fence
when they saw me,
and for once
things were simple—
the soft crunch
of their chewing,
the tiny lights
in the valley,
the mist settling in,
and then, like golden sheep
grazing, the clouds—
suffused with sunlight—
descending
upon the hills.

Unhatched

Every morning
I'd search for eggs
amid the straw
and shit.
When I wiped them off
they gleamed
like treasure,
stolen, unhatched,
full of yolk.

Patterns

Is it possible the sea
came to lap about the edges
of the house while I slept?
The tide higher
than I thought, the cliffs
just rocks under water.

It comes, the tide,
to fill our sleep with dreams.
That's what the ocean is, isn't it?
Full of dreams
that pull, pull, pull us
till we resist no longer.

There is such music
in the sea.
It knows the patterns
of our souls. It knows
that which has
no pattern, yet repeats.

Tell me, Ocean, I asked,
how can I love,
forgive, forgive,
and then
love
again?

Ocean

The water the waves washed ashore
shone mother-of-pearl
on the dark sand.

Life

Light rested its watery hands
on the old maple. Dew
trickled down
along the bark, nuzzled
against moss.

A chorus of cicadas
cleared their scratchy throats
to sing. Lilac flowers yawned open.
Enchanted, my footsteps were soft
as sun rays, just tiptoes
on grass.

Beside me, a black moth
hoisted its wings in the tall blades
like a pair of dark flags
raised to greet the day.

Memory

I cast a net, then waited,
for those old precious moments
to come darting out—
silvery, elusive, eager
to slip back into the mind's ocean,
to lose themselves
among my thoughts.

That's where they belonged,
of course, but when I caught them
they were gleaming still.

That first kiss.
Our walks together.
His nineteenth birthday.

No place for those memories
anymore, so I let them loose,
released them so they could live
in the past, no knowledge
of what's to come,
blissful, untarnished.

Boat Dream

Leaves curled red and orange
toward the water.
I hopped into a rowboat,
took off my shoes and socks.
Bare feet propped up,
the current a steady tug,
I pushed away from shore.

About the Author

Mary McCormack Deka has been published in India and the US. Her poems have appeared in the *Goodreads* newsletter, *Railonama,* and *The Mystic Nebula.* She won the Bare Hands Poetry and Photography Postcard Competition of 2013 and was a recipient of the Quinn Award for Poetry in 2012.

She's inspired by everything—oceans and forests, sardines and tangerines, stained glass and kizomba dancing. She likes to travel, read, write, and tell stories.

Follow her adventures and writing on her website: www.marydeka.com.

www.ingramcontent.com/pod-product-compliance
Lightning Source LLC
Chambersburg PA
CBHW031607040426
42452CB00006B/433